People at Work
Building

Jan Champney *Photographs by* Chris Fairclough

W
FRANKLIN WATTS
LONDON • SYDNEY

First published in 2008 by Franklin Watts
338 Euston Road, London NW1 3BH

Franklin Watts Australia
Level 17/207 Kent Street
Sydney NSW 2000

Copyright © Franklin Watts 2008

All rights reserved.

Editor: Julia Bird
Art Director: Jonathan Hair
Designer: Jane Hawkins
Photography: Chris Fairclough (unless otherwise credited)

Picture credits:
p.9: Shutterstock © Wally Stemberger; p.21: Corbis © Jorn Tomter/zefa/Corbis;
p.23: (top) Shutterstock © Claus Mikosch; (bottom) Shutterstock © Annette;
p.19: (top) istockphoto © Tomas Bercic; (bottom) Shutterstock © Frances A. Miller

Every attempt has been made to clear copyright.
Should there be any inadvertent omission please
apply to the publisher for rectification.

A CIP catalogue record for this book
is available from the British Library

ISBN: 978 0 7496 7821 0

Dewey Classification: 362.1

Printed in China

Franklin Watts is a division of Hachette Children's Books,
an Hachette Livre UK company.

Note to parents and teachers: Every effort has been made by the Publishers to ensure that the websites on p.31 of this book are suitable for children, that they are of the highest educational value, and that they contain no inappropriate or offensive material. However, because of the nature of the Internet, it is impossible to guarantee that the contents of these sites will not be altered. We strongly advise that Internet access is supervised by a responsible adult.

Contents

Construction	4
On the drawing board	6
Planning it out	8
Groundwork	10
Organising the site	12
On-site workers	14
Up in the sky	16
Inside job	18
Kit it out	20
Wire it up	22
Water works	24
The finishing touches	26
Other builders	28
Glossary	30
Skills and training	31
Index	32

Construction

The cities, towns and villages around us are very important. They are where we live, go to work and enjoy free time.

Think about the place where you live.

- Do you live in a city with lots of blocks of flats?
- Or in a small town or village with mostly houses?
- Are you close to the sea or countryside?
- How far do you travel to go shopping or to school?

A village high street.

High-rise buildings are more common in a city than in a small town or village.

Now think about the buildings, bridges, tunnels and roads in your city, town or village. All of these **structures** have been designed and built by people in the **construction industry**.

Bridges are large structures that transport people over waterways, roads and railways.

The construction industry employs people of all ages.

Construction is a huge industry that employs more than 2.2 million people in Britain. There are many different kinds of jobs to do in construction and all of them play a part in making the houses, offices, shops and roads that people use every day.

? Key Questions

Do you know anyone who works in the construction industry?

What do they do?

On the drawing board

Before it is built, every building and structure starts out as an idea. The people who turn these ideas into drawings are called **architects**.

Architects spend a lot of their time working indoors at a computer or desk. Their job is to make plans and drawings that show what the finished building or structure should look like. They also give advice about which materials should be used to build it.

This architect is finishing off the floor plan for a housing development.

Architects' plans
Architects use particular tools to draw up detailed building plans. These include set squares and special desks called drafting tables. Today, most architects also use architectural computer software to help them draw up building plans.

Architects often carry out site visits to make sure their plans are being followed.

Linda is an architect. She explains:

"Once I have designed the plans and the **client** is happy, I visit the builders and engineers on **site**. I check that my drawings are being followed and make any changes that my client wants. I became an architect because I enjoyed art and design and technology so much at school. It helps to like maths, too."

? Key Questions

Why do you think art and design and technology are useful subjects to study if you want to be an architect?

What things do you think the architect has to consider when designing a structure?

Planning it out

Before construction on a building project can begin, the client needs to consult a **planning officer** and a **surveyor**.

There are special laws in place to ensure that the buildings and other structures around us are safe to live in or use and are right for their local **environment**. Planning officers make sure that these laws are kept to.

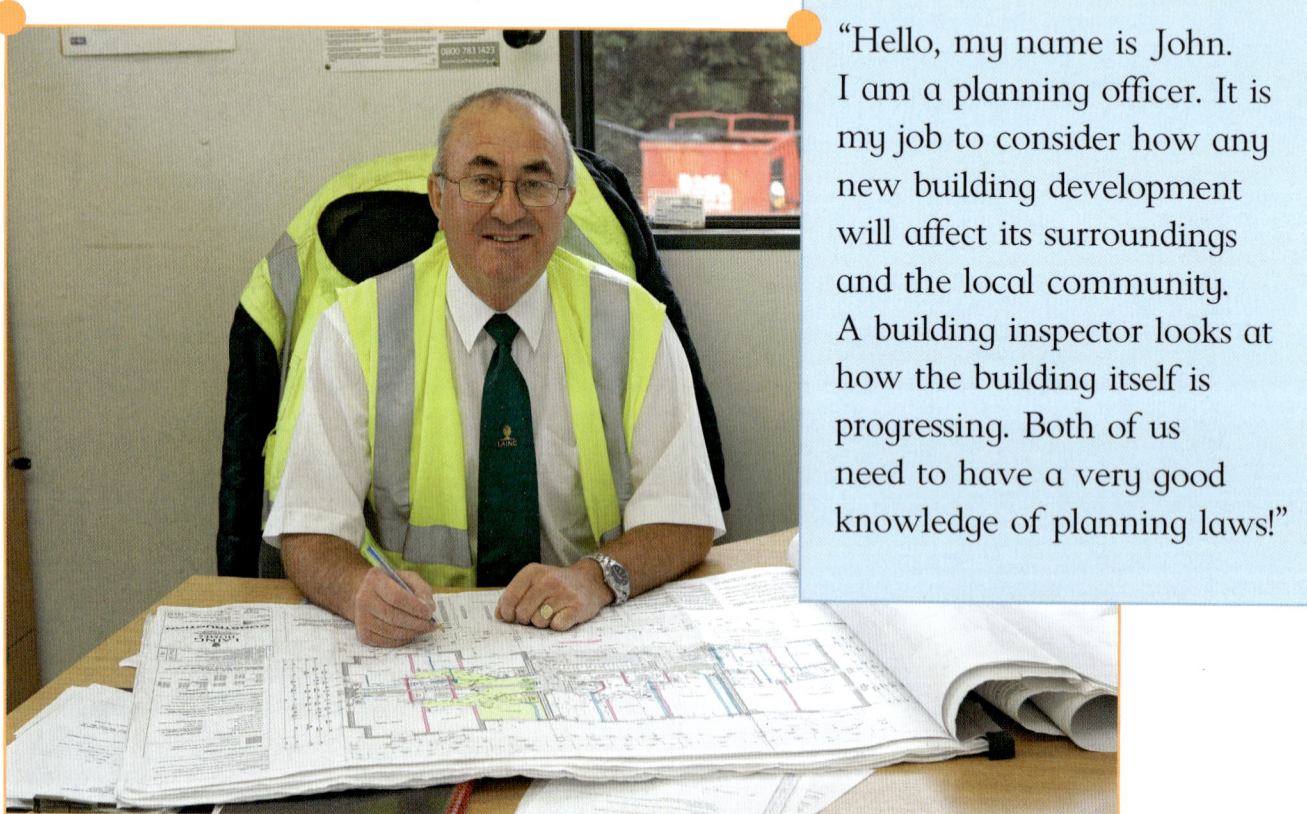

"Hello, my name is John. I am a planning officer. It is my job to consider how any new building development will affect its surroundings and the local community. A building inspector looks at how the building itself is progressing. Both of us need to have a very good knowledge of planning laws!"

Planning officers also help to obtain permission for any new building development before construction begins, and carry out site visits.

A surveyor offers advice and guidance on all aspects of building. There are lots of different kinds of surveyor. They help their clients to make the most of their land or property.

This surveyor is using a mechanical measuring wheel. It clicks when it has travelled a certain distance.

Surveyors

Each surveyor is an expert in a different area. These include:

- Measuring pieces of land using **specialist** equipment.
- Giving advice to people about how best to use their land.
- Telling people how much their homes and land are worth.
- Working out the cost of building projects.

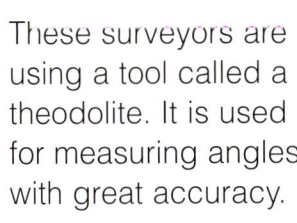

These surveyors are using a tool called a theodolite. It is used for measuring angles with great accuracy.

Groundwork

Before new building work starts, every site has to be prepared. This is called **groundwork**. It is done by a team of surveyors, **engineers**, labourers and **plant** drivers.

First, the engineers work out what is needed and where it should go. They use special measuring equipment to mark out the layout of the new building.

Safety check
Construction engineers are responsible for making sure that each stage in a building project is carried out safely, correctly and on time. To do this, they survey the land, look at reports and test the building materials.

Before construction can begin, engineers use measuring equipment to check that the ground is level.

Foundations

New buildings are built on special beds made of concrete or steel called **footings**. These make up a building's **foundations**. Laying them is heavy and dusty work.

When the footings have been laid, the engineers check everything is level. When they are happy, the building can be built.

The labourers and plant drivers dig up and level the soil to prepare for building. They use heavy machines such as **excavators** to do this.

A pipelayer at work.

Buildings are supplied with gas and water by pipes that run under the ground. When a new building is built, new pipes must be laid. This work is done by skilled workers called pipelayers.

Organising the site

Mark (right) is a construction project manager.

A good project manager will take time to talk to a member of his team.

Key Questions

What skills do you think a project manager should have?

Why do you think project managers have usually worked in the industry for a long time?

Mark says:
"My job is to keep the site safe. I also plan the work and make sure everything keeps to schedule. I order the building materials and check the deliveries. I also look after the construction team and help with any problems they have, so it helps to be a good listener."

The project manager is supported by a big workforce during construction. The plant drivers use and drive the special tools and vehicles such as excavators, cranes, diggers and bulldozers.

A plant driver transports some earth away from the site.

Rules of the site
If you visit a construction and building site you will see signs and rules on display. People who work in the construction industry need to think about their own safety, as well as the safety of the people they are working with and the general public.

On-site workers

On a building site, the plant drivers help to dig the footings and do all the jobs that would be difficult without the help of a machine. Labourers help out with the work.

Jonathan and Adrian are labourers. "Our job is to help the others in any way we're asked and every day is different. One day we might knock down a wall, the next we could be helping the bricklayers by mixing and pouring concrete. Labourers help to keep the site clean and tidy, too. It helps to be fit and to like being outdoors! It's also a real advantage to be a good team player."

Mark is helping to plaster some walls.

Bricklaying is one of the most common on-site construction jobs.

Brian is a bricklayer. He builds brick walls but also works with other materials, such as breeze blocks, tiles and concrete. He cuts and works out how many bricks are needed for each job. He uses a tool called a trowel to spread the **mortar** that holds the bricks together.

Brian says:
"I am out in all types of weather. It can be hot and dusty in the summer and very cold and wet in the winter. But seeing the finished building makes it all worthwhile."

Other site workers

It takes a big team of workers to keep a construction site going. Other jobs on site include:

- forklift truck driver
- **welder**
- **stonemason**
- equipment maintenance worker.

Up in the sky

Some construction involves working at heights. **Scaffolding** is put up around buildings and structures that are being constructed so that builders can do work high up on a building.

Robert puts up and takes down scaffolding. It can be dangerous work.

Robert says:
"New buildings can be hundreds of metres high. When we put up the scaffolding, we have to be careful not to drop things below us or slip. When it's up we check everything is safe and secure. When the building work is finished, we take the scaffolding back down. You can't be afraid of heights doing this job!"

Safety first

Working at heights can be dangerous, particularly when the weather is wet or windy. Roofers and tilers have to take great care when working and wear protective clothing, such as hard hats, luminous vests and, if necessary, safety harnesses.

These roofers are making a wooden frame for the roof. When it is complete, they will put a layer of felt over it and then add a layer of tiles.

Roofers work in all weathers and use special safety equipment to protect them. They work on both **restoring** old roofs and building new ones. They can work on their own or in a team and have to trust each other. Roofers are trained to use a variety of different materials in their work, such as tiles, felt and slate.

Inside job

Most of the people we have met so far build the outside structure of a building, but people who work on the inside of a building are just as important to the construction industry.

There are workers who make buildings warm, dry and comfortable to live in by supplying them with electricity, water and gas. Others paint and decorate the interior, and fit doors, windows and carpets.

Once a bathroom has been built, it needs to be plastered, tiled and fitted with plumbing for the toilet and bath.

Fixtures and fittings, such as lighting, carpets and windows change the appearance of any building or structure.

As well as decorating and installing electricity, heating and plumbing in a building, workers also need to **maintain** these systems. This can mean checking and servicing equipment, replacing old or worn parts and dealing with emergencies such as power cuts or burst pipes.

Electricians fit and maintain fuse boxes. These contain the fuses that regulate a building's electricity.

Key Questions

What does a building need to make it a nice place to live in?

What features make a town or village a good place to live?

Apprenticeship

As in many industries, construction workers often start off as **apprentices** to more experienced workers. They perform simple tasks under the supervision of the worker they are apprenticed to. In return, they are able to learn the trade on the job.

Kit it out

An important next step is fitting a building's windows, doors and stairs. This is work done by window fitters and carpenters.

These window fitters are installing a set of French windows.

In an old building, a window fitter will first remove any old windows with powerful tools. He will then measure up the space for the new windows before installing them. He secures the new windows with powerful glue to make them weatherproof.

Chris (right) is an apprentice window fitter.
"I work outdoors most of the time in a team. We fit windows, doors and sometimes conservatories. We need to measure them up very carefully. Once the glass is in place, we have to make sure it is all level and secure, so that the glass won't leak. We use different equipment, including special suction tools to help us carry the glass around. We need to be pretty careful doing that, too!"

Fittings, such as doors and wooden window frames, are designed and built by a carpenter.

Carpenters measure, cut, sand and join wood using special tools and equipment. Some make doors, windows and stairs. Others design and make furniture. Their tools are sharp and dangerous so carpenters have to know how to use them safely. They are trained to know about different types of wood and which wood is best for each job.

Carpentry tools

Carpenters use special measuring and levelling tools to make sure their wood is cut to the correct length, that it is smooth and that the joins are level. To make sure the pieces are being put together correctly the carpenter uses a tool called a **spirit level** (right).

Wire it up

Electricity provides lighting and powers electrical appliances. In some homes, it is also used to provide heating. Electricity is therefore essential for almost every new building or structure.

There are different types of electrician. Richard is a trainee domestic electrician. He helps to wire new buildings and repair old electrical systems. A lot of his work takes place indoors.

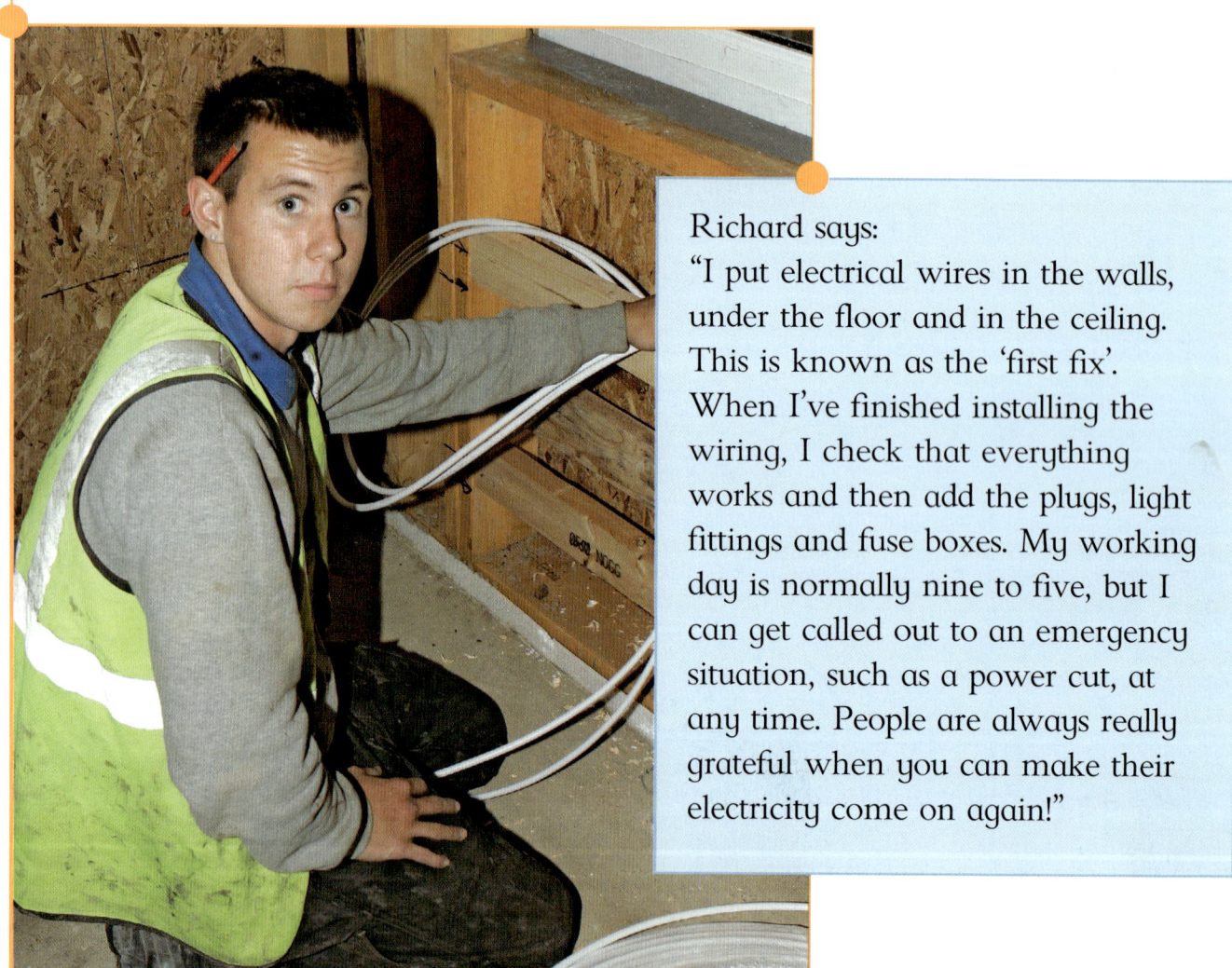

Richard says:
"I put electrical wires in the walls, under the floor and in the ceiling. This is known as the 'first fix'. When I've finished installing the wiring, I check that everything works and then add the plugs, light fittings and fuse boxes. My working day is normally nine to five, but I can get called out to an emergency situation, such as a power cut, at any time. People are always really grateful when you can make their electricity come on again!"

Other electricians work directly for a construction company as part of a team. They can work all over the world on large-scale projects, such as building a new sports stadium or an airport terminal.

Electricians can work on huge construction sites, as well as in the home.

Alert to danger
Working with electricity can be dangerous, so electricians have to take great care and follow strict health and safety rules. These include maintaining their tools to high standards and wearing protective clothing, such as hard hats and rubber boots.

Water works

Water is needed in every home for cooking, washing, flushing toilets, watering gardens and more. Putting in and maintaining a building's plumbing system is a major job and requires a lot of training and experience.

In the home, plumbers fit bathrooms, mend leaking pipes, clear blockages and plumb in household appliances such as washing machines and dishwashers. They have to be able to follow plans and diagrams, and must also stick to building regulations.

Working for themselves
Many construction workers, such as plumbers and electricians, are **self-employed**. This means that they have to find their own work and do their own accounts, but it also means that they can work when and where they want to.

Steve is a plumber. He works mainly in people's homes, installing and maintaining hot and cold water systems.

Steve bends pipe work using one of his tools.

Steve says:
"I put in heating and water systems and new bathrooms. I follow the architect's drawings by putting in pipe work which I install using bending and measuring tools. I heat the joins and make sure there aren't any leaks. I learned my trade by doing a course at college. During my training, I did work experience with a qualified plumber. When I finished my course, he offered me a job. I stayed with the company for three years before deciding to become my own boss."

Saving water

It is important to save water at home whenever possible. Plumbers can help by mending leaking taps, maintaining old pipes and fitting water-saving devices to taps, toilets, pipes and showers.

The finishing touches

Once the main construction work on a building or structure is finished, it is time to decorate! This is the work of plasterers, painters and decorators and floor and carpet layers.

Pete (left) and Graham are painters and decorators. They paint or wallpaper the insides and outsides of homes and businesses.

Pete says:
"First, I meet the client to discuss the project and to work out what materials will be needed. Before I start work, I make sure any surfaces in the room are covered up. Then I strip and rub down the walls before painting or hanging the wallpaper. I often have to work on a ladder or scaffolding, so it's good that I don't mind heights!"

This decorator is smoothing out new plaster.

There are lots of different types of flooring for homes and workplaces. You can choose between carpets, wood, vinyl, laminate and tiles. The people who lay floors are carpet fitters and floor layers. They work out how much flooring is needed, give advice about which type to use and then lay it.

Carpet fitters
Carpet fitters travel to homes and businesses fitting and laying carpets. They use cutting tools to cut the carpet cleanly.

Floor layers
Floor layers lay floors using materials such as laminate, wood, slate and tiles. They may repair old floor surfaces to make them even before they start work. They use materials such as glue and cement to keep the flooring in place.

Floor layers can help clients to decide which kind of flooring will suit their home or office best.

? Key Questions

Industrial painters and decorators can work on big structures such as ships or bridges. What skills do you think you need for this kind of work?

Other builders

Not everyone in the construction industry works on a building site.

Some builders work on our homes to improve or **renovate** them or to help them to save energy.

Ian helps to keep homes and offices warm by helping to **insulate** them.

Ian says:
"My job helps people to save energy and money! I add insulating material into the walls and roofs of buildings. The material helps to insulate the building by keeping the heat in. This is good news for homeowners. Their fuel bills become lower as they use less power to heat their homes. Saving energy also helps to reduce **climate change**."

Insulating your home can reduce heat loss by up to 30%.

Other types of builders work in transport construction. Many work under the ground to build and maintain tunnels for underground trains. This work often takes place at night when the trains are not in use.

It is important to work as a team underground where it can be cold and dark.

Andy is a road worker. He builds and repairs roads and motorways. Safety is very important in this job.

Andy says:
"We put up warning signs and brightly coloured cones to warn drivers that we are working on the road. We also redirect the traffic away from us. Roadworks can slow traffic down, so we have to work as quickly as we can — including at night!"

Andy is helping to lay a new road surface.

Key Questions

What other kinds of building projects can you think of? Can you name some of the jobs that there might be in these projects?

Glossary

Apprentices People who work alongside more experienced workers to learn a trade.

Architects People who design and oversee the construction of a building or structure.

Client Someone who pays someone to do a job for them.

Climate change A gradual change in the world's climate.

Construction industry The job family for building work.

Engineers People who use science in their work. Engineers work in a variety of industries.

Environment Surroundings.

Excavators Power diggers.

Footings The base of a building or structure, also known as **foundations**.

Groundwork The preparation of a site for a new building or structure.

Insulate To keep heat in and cold out of a building or structure by adding a layer of material around it, for example in the walls.

Maintain To keep in a state of good repair.

Mortar A mixture of cement and other materials that sticks building materials, such as bricks, together.

Planning officer Someone who makes sure a new building or structure follows local planning laws and is safe to live or work in.

Plant Digging and lifting equipment such as cranes, diggers and bulldozers.

Renovate To do work on a building to return it to an earlier or better condition.

Restoring Returning something, for example a building, to an earlier or better condition.

Scaffolding A temporary frame built around a building or structure so people can work on high parts.

Self-employed Working for yourself, rather than for a company.

Site A place where something is located, for example a building site.

Specialist Used for a particular job.

Spirit level A tool used in carpentry and building.

Stonemason Someone who works or builds with stone.

Structure Something that has been constructed, such as a bridge or a stadium. Buildings are also structures.

Surveyor Someone who advises and assists with many stages of construction. There are many different types of surveyor.

Welder Someone who joins pieces of metal together using special tools.

Skills and training

You now know that the construction industry has lots of different jobs on offer.

Many need special skills and training. You can develop these skills by going to college or university. However, there are some jobs that can be done with only a small amount of training.

Training and qualifications table

Architect Surveyor	Degree
Planning officer Construction manager	2-3 A-levels NVQ Level 3 Level 3 Diploma
Electrician Plumber	4-5 GCSEs (Grades A-C) NVQ Level 2 Level 2 Diploma
Painter and decorator Carpet fitter Bricklayer Carpenter	GCSEs (Grades D-F) NVQ Level 1 Level 1 Diploma
Groundworker Plant driver Labourer Scaffolder Window fitter	Few or no qualifications

The table above shows the normal minimum qualifications needed for each job. There will be times when more or fewer qualifications are needed, so use the table only as a guide!

The courses you can take depend on what is on offer in your area. Ask your careers teacher or contact Connexions (www.connexions-direct.com) for advice.

Further information

For more information on building and construction contact the following organisations:

ConstructionSkills
CITB-ConstructionSkills
Tel: 01485 577577
Email: information.centre@cskills.org
www.citb-constructionskills.co.uk

Federation of Master Builders
Tel: 020 7242 7583
www.fmb.org.uk

National Access and Scaffolding Confederation
Tel: 020 7397 8120
Email: enquiries@nasc.org.uk
www.nasc.org.uk

Royal Institute of Chartered Surveyors
Tel: 0870 333 1600
Email: contactrics@rics.org
www.rics.org

Royal Institute of Chartered Surveyors-Scotland
Tel: 0131 225 7078
Email: scot@rics.org.uk
www.rics.org/scotland

Royal Town Planning Institute
Tel: 020 7929 9494
www.rtpi.org.uk

Royal Town Planning Institute in Scotland
Tel: 0131 226 1959
www.rtpi.org.uk/rtpi_in_scotland/

SummitSkills
Tel: 01908 303960
Email: enquiries@summitskills.org.uk
www.summitskills.org.uk

Index

apprentices 19, 20, 30
architects 6, 7, 25, 30, 31

bricklayers 14, 15, 31
bridges 5, 27
builders 7, 28, 29
building inspectors 8
building regulations 24
building sites 7, 8, 10, 13, 14, 15, 23, 28
bulldozers 13

carpenters 20, 21, 31
carpets and carpet laying 18, 26, 27, 31
clients 7, 8, 9, 26, 27
climate change 28
college 25, 31
computers 6
conservatories 20
construction industry 5, 13, 30
construction project managers 12-13, 31
construction sites (see building sites)
cranes 13

diggers 13
doors 18, 20, 21
drafting tables 6

electricians 19, 22, 23, 24, 31
electricity 11, 18, 19, 22, 23
emergencies 19, 22
energy 28
engineers 7, 10, 11
environment 8, 30
equipment 9, 10, 19, 20, 21
equipment maintenance workers 15
excavators 11, 13

fixtures and fittings 18, 21
flats 4
floors and floor laying 22, 26, 27
footings 11, 14, 30
forklift truck drivers 15
foundations 11, 30
furniture 21
fuse boxes 19, 22

gas 11, 18
groundwork 10, 30, 31

heating 19, 22, 25
high-rise buildings 4
houses 4, 5, 6

insulation 28, 30

labourers 10, 11, 14, 31
land 9, 10
laws 8
leaks 20, 24, 25
lighting 18, 22

maintenance 19, 24, 25, 30
materials 6, 10, 12, 15, 17, 26, 27

offices 5, 27, 28

painting and decorating 18, 19, 26, 27, 31
pipelayers 11
pipes 11, 19, 24, 25
planning officers 8, 30, 31
planning permission 8
plans 6, 7, 24
plant drivers 10, 11, 13, 14, 31
plasterers and plastering 18, 26
plumbers 24, 25, 31
plumbing 18, 19, 24

protective clothing 17, 23

qualifications 31

renovation 28, 30
restoration 17, 30
roads 5, 29
roofers 17
rules 13

safety 10, 12, 13, 16, 17, 21, 23, 29
scaffolding 16, 26, 30, 31
schedule 12
school 4, 7
  subjects 7
self-employed 24, 30
shops 4, 5
skills 12, 27, 31
spirit level 21, 30
stairs 20, 21
stonemasons 15, 30
surveyors 8, 9, 10, 30, 31

tiles and tiling 15, 17, 18, 27
tools 6, 9, 13, 20, 21, 23, 25, 27
towns 4, 5, 19
training 24, 25, 31
transport 5, 29
tunnels 5, 29

villages 4, 5, 19

wallpaper 26
water 11, 18, 24, 25
  saving 25
weather 15, 17, 20
welders 15, 30
windows and window fitters 18, 20, 21, 31
wiring 22
work experience 25